# SNEFRU

## PHARAOH OF THE 4TH DYNASTY

Leaders of the Ancient World

# SNEFRU

## PHARAOH OF THE 4TH DYNASTY

Beatriz Santillian and
Susanna Thomas

Rosen YA™
New York

*For Madeleine Reichman —BS*
*For Perran and Laura Thomas —ST*

Published in 2018 by The Rosen Publishing Group, Inc.
29 East 21st Street, New York, NY 10010



First Edition



**Library of Congress Cataloging-in-Publication Data**

Names: Santillian, Beatriz, author. | Thomas, Susanna, 1966– author.
Title: Snefru : Pharaoh of the 4th Dynasty / Beatriz Santillian and Susanna Thomas.
Description: First edition. | New York : Rosen Publishing, [2018] | Series: Leaders of the ancient world | Includes bibliographical references and index. | Audience: Grades 7–12.
Identifiers: LCCN 2016053656 | ISBN 9781508174912 (library bound)
Subjects: LCSH: Sneferu, King of Egypt--Juvenile literature. | Egypt--Civilization--To 332 B.C.--Juvenile literature. | Pharaohs--Biography--Juvenile literature.
Classification: LCC DT85.S65 S25 2016 | DDC 932/.012092 [B] --dc23
LC record available at https://lccn.loc.gov/2016053656

*Manufactured in the United States of America.*

**On the cover**: *Foreground*: Sandstone statue of Snefru that currently resides in the Museum of Egyptian Antiquities in Cairo. *Background*: The Bent Pyramid, located in Dashur, Egypt.

# CONTENTS

# INTRODUCTION

Egypt's most famous attractions are its pyramids. Every pyramid tells the story of the king who had it built. Snefru, the king of Egypt from 2613 to 2589 BCE, used a different approach than his ancestors, and this approach eventually allowed him and his descendants to carry on the new tradition of smooth-sided pyramids.

Snefru wasn't only concerned about constructing a pyramid where his people would rest his body after his death. Even more important than preparing for the afterlife was preparing a successor to take his place. Egyptian pharaohs traditionally reproduced with another member of the royal family. This allowed the royals to keep the throne in family line. Continuing this tradition would give Snefru's sons a legitimate claim to the throne, and would prevent any internal conflicts that might arise from failing to produce an heir.

Snefru also cared about improving his community. He had wood imported for building grandiose boats and commissioned building projects, including a palace in Memphis. He also led a military excursion to keep the nomadic Libyan tribes from damaging or influencing Egypt,

This 1894 Armand Colin map from Atlas Vidal-Lablache depicts ancient Egypt and its prominent geographical features.

although it is now clear that they didn't pose much of a threat to begin with. His invasion of Nubian territory did help finance his pyramids and other projects, and showed his cold, calculating attitude toward sacrificing others to achieve his goals.

Snefru's was a typical Egyptian king who used his intellect and the resources at his disposal to solve crucial problems he discovered during his reign. Before entering into a conflict, he carefully made sure that his troops were better prepared than the enemy. His government's organization was incredibly stable, so they were able to methodologically approach and complete several pyramids—truely massive and demanding building projects. And, he unwaveringly took part in the traditions of his people. These traditions were guiding set of principles that decided much of his life for him.

The mysteries of ancient civilizations can be very difficult to solve. Some records made by the ancient Egyptions, like government reports and wall paintings, have survived the ages and ancient Egyptian scholars can use these to understand this civilization. But many of these artifacts are incomplete, and even a complete artifact may be difficult to interprate—especially when working with a pictorial written language like hieroglyphics.

Snefru himself is shrouded in mysteries. What caused his unsteady resolve towards his most massive building projects, some of which he almost canceled? Why did Snefru feel that a nomadic tribe offered a threat to the stability and wealth of a united Egypt? Scholars may someday uncover more artifacts that can answer some of these questions, or even disprove current theory. The information this book presents about Snefru is the best uderstanding that we have of the paraoh today, but scholarship is always evolving.

CHAPTER 1

# EGYPT IN SNEFRU'S YOUTH

The environment of ancient Egypt during the twenty-sixth century BCE offered Snefru, the son of a king, a clear path to ascension. His upbringing and his education groomed him for the role, and the people around him knew that he was the chosen one. But he had many lessons to learn before he would be ready to lead.

## THE ROYAL PALACE

Snefru's father was King Huni, who was the last pharaoh of the Third Dynasty, and his mother was Meresankh I, who was a royal princess and may have been the sister of Huni. Throughout Egyptian history, it was normal for the pharaoh to marry his own sisters and his own daughters.

We actually know very little about Huni. The

Turin Canon and the Saqqara king list both identify him as the last king of the Third Dynasty and the father of Snefru. His name is also inscribed on a piece of red granite found at Elephantine (near Aswan), suggesting that he built a fortress there on the southern border of Egypt. His tomb has never been positively identified, but it is likely that he was buried either at Meidum in the Faiyum region or at Saqqara near the step pyramid of Djoser.

Snefru was born and grew up in the royal palace in the capital city of Memphis, near modern-day Cairo. We have no evidence of this palace, but comparison with other sources indicates that it would have been a large, luxurious building. The walls were made of mud brick, and the windows were set just below the ceiling in order to let in light and cool breezes. It seldom rained in Memphis, so there would also have been living spaces on the roof, which were probably shaded with canopies made of linen and matting. The palace compound would have included the main buildings, which contained many different suites of rooms, including bedrooms, bathrooms, banqueting halls, and rooms for receiving guests. Some of the rooms would have been open to the sky, perhaps with roofed walkways or colonnades around the edges. The walls and floors of the palace would have been brightly painted with pictures of plants and flowers and geometric patterns. There would have been shallow pools containing water lilies and fish, and gardens full of trees and flowers.

The palace compound would also have housed vegetable gardens, kitchens, and storerooms full of food, as well as a bakery to make bread and cakes and a brewery to make beer, which was the most common drink. There was probably also a butchery area, where animals either from the palace compound or from surrounding country estates would have been slaughtered and cut up in preparation for cooking. There may also have been a potter's workshop to make all the vessels needed for preparing, cooking, and eating food, as well as to provide lamps, big jars to hold water, and other household items. There may well have been a metalworking area for making and mending copper tools used in the house. There would also have been a laundry, and an area for spinning and weaving wool and linen for clothing.

All the work of looking after children, preparing food, cooking, and cleaning would have been

It is clear that this painting from the Tomb of Khaemwaset depicts an ancient Egyptian prince because of his hairstyle, the side ponytail, and his clothing.

done by servants. However, royal women were sometimes involved in making and sewing cloth, as needlework was considered a ladylike task.

## ANCIENT EGYPTIAN EDUCATION

Evidence from later periods suggests that the palace would have been the home for all of the royal women and children, while the pharaoh would have had a number of homes that he used as he traveled around the country. Snefru grew up in an extended family with his mother Meresankh, as well as the other wives of the pharaoh, his brothers and sisters, and probably also various aunts and cousins. He would have gone to school, which was called the "house of instruction," with other boys in the palace compound. There he was taught drawing, painting, mathematics, and reading and writing. There is no evidence that there were specially trained professional schoolteachers during this period, and it is thought that royal uncles and other male relatives probably took charge of instruction at these palace schools. School would have taken place in the morning, as is still the case in Egypt. Many of the lessons would have taken place outdoors in the fine weather. Boys sat cross-legged in rows on the ground.

Although the Egyptians had invented a very fine sort of paper called papyrus that was made out of reeds, it was quite expensive to produce. Consequently, students practiced writing on wooden tablets covered in white paint, as well as on scraps of flat stone and pieces of broken pottery. Snefru was taught both hieratic and hieroglyphic writing. Boys learned to write by copying phrases and exercises. Hieratic was the equivalent of modern handwriting, and it was always written from left to right. Hieroglyphic script consisted of a series of picture symbols and was mainly used to decorate buildings and monuments. Nearly a thousand signs were used during the Old Kingdom. Hieroglyphs were written right to left, left to right, or top to bottom. The signs were written without punctuation or gaps between words, and there were also no vowels. Some signs represented consonants, some represented sounds, and some represented ideas. The Egyptians also loved puns and word games, and many signs have more than one meaning. Most ancient Egyptians couldn't read hieroglyphic writing, but Snefru would have learned at least the basics of the language.

A painted wooden tablet like this would serve as a perfect canvas for an ancient Egyptian student who was learning how to write.

He also learned how to hunt wild animals in the desert, and how to spear fish from a small boat on the Nile. Travel at this time was almost always by water rather than by road, and a canal would have joined the Nile to the palace. He would probably have sailed model boats made of wood or papyrus on the canal, and played games like tug-of-war

# WRITTEN LANGUAGES THROUGH THE AGES

The first type of writing to develop historically was logographic writing. Logographic writing uses symbols to represent whole words or phrases. Pictographic writing is one kind of logographic writing that uses images to represent one idea or object that the image refers to. Some examples of logographic languages are ancient Egyptian hieroglyphics, the Han characters of Chinese, Japanese, Korean, Vietnamese, and Mayan script.

The second writing structure to appear was the syllabary system, in which symbols are meant to represent letters or sounds. Some logographic languages like ancient Egyptian hieroglyphs have a syllabary component that helps guide the flow of the language, or help a reader to pronounce the logographs. And some systems are purely syllabary, offering symbols that only represent sounds that the reader must interpret collectively as ideas. Some exclusively syllabary languages include English, German, Arabic, and Russian (barring the commonly-found Arabic and Roman numerals).

A third system, ideographic writing, unifies languages while encompassing the traits of the pictograph. Analogously, in Chinese writing, a group of people who speak different dialects would be able to understand a

SIDEBAR CONTINUED ON THE NEXT PAGE

SIDEBAR CONTINUED FROM THE PREVIOUS PAGE

written passage. But if either of them reads it out loud, they would not recognize the sounds of other group members. Similarly, ideographic writing offers images that a group of travelers from different countries would all recognize: A stick-figure man and woman indicate bathrooms for men and women, a crossed red circle covering an object or activity, like part of a cigarette, indicates the object or activity is prohibited. This is a more recent application of language concepts with a global audience in mind.

and arm wrestling with his friends. Leather balls have been found that show that boys played various games of catch, and there are also sets of bowling pins from this period. Snefru would have had various wooden toys to play with, as well as a pet hunting dog.

Snefru wore a short, knee-length kilt in the summer, which was tied together around his waist. He may have worn a triangular loincloth as underwear, which again would have been tied together. In the winter he wore a linen shirt as well, and probably a wool or leather cloak. His sandals were made of woven reeds. His hair would have been quite long, and it would have been worn in a plaited bunch on the side of his head. Probably when he was about twelve years old, this "side-lock" was cut off and he was circumcised, both acts indicating that he was no longer considered a child.

## WEAPONS OF WAR

During the Old Kingdom there was no need for a permanent standing army in Egypt. Individual local governors and officials had their own small armies or groups of soldiers who kept order. These soldiers also acted as a sort of police force. They guarded important officials and their families, and there is also evidence that they patrolled the desert around each settlement in order to protect against raids from desert Bedouins. The king and his palace also had a small troop of bodyguards, as well as a special group of officials who guarded the royal women in the palace harem. There was also a group of officials who arrested and punished people for crimes like non-payment of taxes. Local rulers also employed mercenaries from Nubia. These men, known as the Medjay, were famed for their height and strength and were often used as scouts, archers, and light infantry.

This Egyptian tomb wall painting depicts boys wearing the knee-length kilt that was a staple of summer clothing.

It is not known how often Snefru saw his father, King Huni, or how much preparation he was given for becoming a pharaoh. He would have spent a few teenage years either attached to a temple priesthood, where he would further his academic and religious studies, or in the army, where he would learn fighting skills and how to command men. However, it is clear that Snefru trained with the palace guard and learned how to use a variety of weapons. These included the mace, the axe, the bow and arrow, the spear, and the throw stick.

The mace was a simple weapon consisting of a pear-shaped stone head attached to a tapering wooden shaft. It was nevertheless an effective weapon and there are many pictures of Egyptians hitting their enemies over the head with this club. Snefru's axe had a semicircular copper head tied to a wooden handle through holes

When attached to a wooden shaft, this head of a club was a weapon that ancient Egyptian warriors used quite successfully in many of their military campaigns.

in the metal. This was also used in hand-to-hand fighting. His spears had sharp tips made of copper or flint (a kind of hard, sharp stone) attached to a wooden staff, and were designed to be thrown at the enemy. His bow was made of one piece of wood narrowing at each end and strung with a piece of animal gut. His arrows were made from reeds with flint or hardwood points and three feathers at the other end. His throw stick was curved (like a boomerang), and was mainly used for catching birds.

During the Old Kingdom soldiers didn't wear armor. Snefru's only protection was a large rectangular shield made of cowhide stretched over a wooden frame. This shield had handles carved in the frame and a leather strap so that it could be hung over his shoulders. However, he was pretty safe practicing with the palace troops because they would all have been very careful not to injure the future king of Egypt.

CHAPTER 2

# SUCCEEDING KING HUNI

Becoming the next pharaoh involved a few steps: choosing new names, starting a family, and strengthening ties to royalty to preserve the dynasty. Just as Snefru had a clear path to becoming the pharaoh because of his upbringing, there were also clear expectations on how to gain the acceptance of the people. Strangely enough, some Egyptian customs also worked to establish particularly strong differences between the actions of the royalty and those of the common people.

## THE KING'S NEW IDENTITY

After ruling for twenty-four years, King Huni died in 2584 BCE. Snefru became king upon the death of his father Huni, and it is thought that he ascended to the throne of Egypt in either his late teens or early twenties. One important step in his coronation was choosing his royal names.

Snefru, like all other Egyptians, received his first name when he was born. However, when he became king he needed new names to express his identity as king. These new names distinguished him from ordinary human beings, and in one sense they acted exactly like his crowns and his robes of state by symbolizing his high status and royal authority. These names were accompanied by special royal titles—Horus, He of the Two Ladies, Horus of Gold, King of Upper and Lower Egypt, and Son of Re.

The title Horus identified the king as an incarnation of the falcon god Horus, who was god of the sky and also the embodiment of divine kingship. Egyptian kings were known as the living Horus. The second title, He of Two Ladies, represented the cobra goddess Wadjet of Buto in the Delta and the vulture goddess Nekbet of El-Kab near Luxor. These two towns were major royal centers from the late predynastic period onward, and this title emphasized the dual nature of Egypt. The third title, Horus of Gold, also showed the godlike nature of the king by associating his name with gold, which

# ANCIENT EGYPTIAN SYMBOLISM

The function of ancient Egyptian symbolism was to emphasize the relationship of Egyptian figures to religion and power. Images or hieroglyphs in writings and art did this through graphic depictions of specific objects. Images that depicted animals often represented gods. For example, Nekhbet, the goddess of Nekheb,

As is common in much of ancient Egyptian art, symbolic as well as personified references to many gods are present and associate the pharaoh with divinity.

was often depicted as a vulture, and Anubis, the god of mummification, was embodied in a jackal or jackal-headed man. Even individual body parts, like an eye, had meaning. The left eye represented the moon, or the eye of Horus, while the right represented the Sun, or the eye of Re. The eye, in particular, had even more significance, as it also represented protection or an offering.

Images of other parts of nature also had symbolic meanings: the sun disk represented Horus, and the plants papyrus and lotus represented lower and upper Egypt, respectively. And objects tend to represent abstract ideas, like *shen*, a circle that both protects and has no beginning or ending. Of course, outside of these, there are numerous other symbols in ancient Egyptian art.

is yellow like the sun and eternal like the flesh of the gods. The fourth title again shows the dual nature of Egypt as represented by two symbols, the sedge (Upper Egypt) and the bee (Lower Egypt). The fifth title, Son of Re, shows a direct divine origin for the king as the child of the sun god.

In later periods the particular identity and

interests of the king were often reflected in the names the new ruler selected. Snefru chose "Lord of Maat" for both his Horus name and his He of Two Ladies name. We do not know if he had a Horus of Gold name or a King of Upper and Lower Egypt name, and it is possible that he used these titles on their own. His Son of Re name, the one by which he had been best known, remained Snefru.

## BUILDING A ROYAL FAMILY

Snefru's main wife, whom he probably married before ascending the throne, was a princess called Hetepheres. She was also the daughter of his father Huni, although they had different mothers. He also had other wives, including daughters of Egyptian nobles and possibly also other of his sisters. It is known that he had at least three sons, called Khufu, Nefermaat, and Rahotep, and also many daughters, including one called Merytyetes.

Ordinary Egyptians did not usually marry their blood relatives, such as brothers marrying sisters or fathers marrying daughters. However, there is a lot of evidence that pharaohs often

This granodiorite statue located in the Museum of Fine Arts in Boston depicts the family of an ancient Egyptian official named Ukhhotep II who served during the New Kingdom.

married royal princesses who were their sisters, and sometimes their daughters. There are many reasons why this was acceptable to the Egyptians.

One reason was that the pharaoh's main wife, who was called the "great royal consort," often played important roles in state festivals and religious ceremonies. A royal princess would have been trained from an early age on how to do these jobs. It is clear, however, that such marriages were more than just symbolic, as one of the main roles of the royal wife was to give the pharaoh an heir, and there are many examples of the pharaoh and his sister/wife or daughter/wife having children.

There were various advantages for the pharaoh in marrying women of the royal family. Children born from these marriages would be doubly royal, and so would have the strongest claim to the throne. Snefru and his sister/wife Hetepheres had a daughter called Merytyetes and a son called Khufu who married each other, and Khufu went on to inherit the throne from his father. Marrying Egyptian princesses and princes also prevented princesses from marrying members of the Egyptian nobility or foreign royalty who might then try to claim the Egyptian throne.

Another reason that the royal family practiced marriage like this was to show that they were like the gods of Egypt. Incest commonly occurred in the myths of Egyptian gods. The main "holy family" consisted of the gods Osiris, Isis, and Horus. Osiris and Isis were brother and sister who married each other, and the pharaoh was the symbolic version of their son Horus on Earth.

In the same way, a "great royal wife" who was the daughter of a pharaoh would have been the daughter of a god. If she married her brother she would be the wife of a god, and if they had children, who become heirs to the throne, she would also be the mother of gods. Consequently, the practice of incest may have been another way of setting the king and his family high above his Egyptian subjects.

As a final note, it is worth remembering that although Egyptian princesses often married their brothers, the pharaohs, pharaohs also had many other wives, some coming from their own family, some from other important Egyptian families, and still others who were the daughters of foreign rulers.

## OTHER EGYPTIAN MARRIAGES

The ancient Egyptians did not have weddings in the way that we know them today. There is no evidence that they had any sort of marriage ceremony—from the richest people to the poorest, marriage was simply achieved by two people setting up house together. Marriages were often arranged by parents, who would have wanted to gain the best possible partners for their children. First cousins often married each other in order to keep property within a family.

Because women sometimes owned their own property, rich couples often signed written contracts deciding how the property would be divided and what would happen if they separated. Divorce was quite common, in which case a woman was either given back any property brought to a marriage, or was compensated in some way. There was also sometimes a distinction

This tomb portrait in the necropolis of the nobles at Thebes depicts a young couple.

between couples who lived together and those who were married. Men usually had only one wife at a time, although some rich men sometimes also had harems.

Evidence from poetry, stories, and illustrations of everyday life shows that the Egyptians thought that to be married with children was the normal way of life, and the one that made people happy.

CHAPTER 3

# AN OLD CUSTOM FOR A NEW KING

The Old Kingdom and Middle Kingdom each constructed of pyramids as the burial places for kings. While a pyramid had many purposes, the most practical was as an eternal resting place for the king. Such pyramids had to be completed before the king's death. Snefru had much to plan and oversee when plotting his own pyramid.

## PREPARING FOR DEATH

Early in his reign, Snefru decided that he would follow the tradition started by his Third Dynasty ancestor Djoser and build a pyramid to be buried in. Snefru was the greatest pyramid builder in Egyptian history and, for reasons that are not clear, ended up constructing not one but three pyramids during his lifetime. Although we have no trace of

Snefru's body, it is thought that he was probably buried in the last pyramid that was built, the Red Pyramid at Dahshur.

His first pyramid was built at Meidum, which is near the mouth of the Faiyum River. It is not known why Snefru chose this site, which is much farther south than previous royal burial sites at Saqqara. However, it is possible that Snefru was fond of the area and that this was already the site of one of his palaces.

During the Old Kingdom, the pharaohs were buried in an area now called the Memphite Necropolis, which spreads along the edge of the desert west of modern-day Cairo. When talking about pyramids, it is important to remember that they were not just single, isolated structures. Each pyramid was surrounded by a small town.

This photo shows the pyramid at Meidum, a step pyramid that resembles the previous work of King Djoser.

A "pyramid complex" included a number of features. There was the main pyramid, of course, and the mortuary temple attached to the base of the pyramid where priests said prayers and brought offerings of food and drink every day for the *Ka*, or soul, of the dead king. There were smaller "satellite" pyramids around the main pyramid where the pharaoh's wives were buried. A valley temple, built by the bank of a canal cut from the river Nile, was where the body of the dead king was first brought from the capital of Memphis. It was also the location of a number of statues of the dead king, so that people who were not allowed into the mortuary temple could still make offerings to him. A causeway linked the valley temple to the mortuary temple. There were rows of *mastaba* tombs, rectangular buildings named after the Arabic word for bench, where less important members of the pharaoh's family, courtiers, and government officials were buried. These tombs were usually given away as presents by the king, and there was probably stiff competition for them as most people wanted to be as close as possible to the king. There was also a village where all the priests and officials who looked after the everyday running of the temples lived.

And there was a small palace for the king to stay in when he came to see how the construction was progressing.

## MANAGING PYRAMID CONSTRUCTION

In order to build each of his pyramids, Snefru commissioned a person to act as "overseer of all the King's works." It was this person's responsibility to organize the quarrying and transportation of huge quantities of stone blocks. These were limestone blocks quarried locally. The best quality blocks of stone were brought from a large quarry at Tura on the east bank of the Nile near Memphis. These were smoothed and polished to a high shine before being used both as the outer casing of the pyramids and to line the walls of the rooms inside.

We are not completely sure how the stone was dug out of the hillsides. The most likely method was one where squares were first drawn on the side or top of the rock and each block was then dug around using hard stone tools, perhaps made of flint. When most of the sides had been freed from the rock face, the block was levered away with wooden poles. Another theory is that small grooves were cut around all the visible sides of the block with handheld copper chisels banged in by hard stone hammers. Wooden wedges were then driven into these grooves and soaked with water, which made the wood expand and so split the piece of stone away from the face of the rock.

Each stone was then hauled away from the quarry on a wooden sledge. Once the stone arrived

Pictured here is the mastaba tomb of Seshemnufer IV (*center*), located south of the Great Pyramid of Giza (*left*) and its satellite pyramid (*right*).

at the site of the pyramid, either by being dragged overland or brought by barges along the river, the sides and edges were chiseled smooth and the stone was put into place.

## LAYING DOWN THE STONES

There is a lot of debate today as to how the pyramids were constructed. Archaeological work at the

Bent Pyramid at Dahshur shows that the pyramid was built straight onto the desert sand. The great weight of the stones meant that the sand started shifting and sinking, which no doubt contributed to the cracking of the building. For the Red Pyramid a foundation platform of several layers of white limestone was first laid down.

The most likely method of construction was one where stones were pulled and pushed up a ramp or ramps that were built against the face of the pyramid. There are many different suggestions as to what type of ramp was used. These include a single straight ramp against one side, a spiral ramp following the four sides, a ramp that zigzagged up one side, or perhaps a combination of some of the above ideas. Such a ramp would have been made out of limestone chips and some sort of plaster to hold the chips together.

The individual blocks would have been pulled up a ramp by a group of men holding ropes tied around the blocks. They may also have been pushed from below. The blocks were probably sitting on wooden tracks (like a railroad), soaked with buckets of water to make them slippery, and may themselves have sat on wooden sledges. The

This painting speculates on whether slave labor or free labor went into building the pyramids.

stones were then laid in horizontal layers with the outermost stone carved with a sloping face along one edge. The pyramid was completed with a single pyramid-shaped stone, known today as the capstone or pyramidion.

## A PYRAMID'S PURPOSE

The first and most obvious reason that the pyramids were built was that they were an enormous visible sign of the wealth and power of the pharaohs. When Snefru built his pyramids they were the biggest man-made stone buildings in the world. If you visit the pyramids today, the first thing you would notice is their size.

Egyptians also thought that the pharaoh's body would be eternally safe hidden in a pyramid. Under the ancient Egyptian belief system the pharaoh's mummified body had to remain untouched on Earth in order to pass into the afterlife. Sadly, this turned out not to be the case, as nearly all the pyramids were robbed soon after completion, probably by the workmen who had helped build them in the first place!

The pyramids also served various religious purposes. The Egyptians had a number of differ-

## INSIDE THE PYRAMID

While a tourist or scientist can visit, pyramids aren't the most accessible of places, due to their hidden chambers. But there have been some recent advances in how to discover those chambers. One method in particular, infrared thermography, seems to present a reliable means of determining the interior of places that the naked eye can't see. It works by scanning an area and looking for notable differences in temperature changes over time. Based on what is known to be there, such differences indicate a significantly dissimilar structure throughout a pyramid. This may mean that the pyramid is made of different materials, or it may mean that there are cavities in which the open air's temperature would not resemble that of the building materials. You may remember from science class that air is usually cooler than land. Until these structures are confirmed, though, what those differences mean is just speculation.

ent religious beliefs and myths, not all of which made sense when taken together. This was mainly because they liked to hang on to old ideas even when new ones appeared. One of the creation myths of Egyptian religion was that the world first rose out of waters called Nun as a mound or hill. The sun, in the form of the sun god Re, was born on this mound, and so day began. It is possible that the pyramids may have represented this mound.

There were three forms of rebirth available to the pharaoh in the Old Kingdom, and these were all linked to the construction of the pyramids. The first, associated with the idea that the king was a living incarnation of the god Horus, had him going to the underworld ruled by Osiris. The second, associated with the sun god Re, had the dead king reborn each morning, traveling with the sun in his ship across the sky, disappearing at night and then reappearing the next morning. The third had the king ascending to the heavens each night to join the stars, but living in his pyramid during the day so as to receive the prayers and offerings brought by the Ka, or soul, from priests in charge of the temple.

## THE HISTORY OF THE PYRAMID

The first pyramid was built during the Third Dynasty by King Djoser (2638–2619 BCE) and was made with a series of steps rather than sloping sides. It is possible that this was meant to be a giant staircase for the pharaoh to climb up to heaven so he could become a star. True pyramids with sloping sides had a pyramidion, a large stone that formed

The first pyramid still stands today in Saqqara, Egypt. It predates the similar-looking pyramid structures of Latin America by about 1,600 years.

the pointed top of the pyramid. These were often golden, and it is thought that the pyramids represented the sloping rays of the sun. Another version of this idea is that the pyramid was the highest object and so the first to great the sun's rays every morning. The biggest pyramid ever built was made by Snefru's son Khufu. This is known as the Great Pyramid and was built at Giza. Each of the four sides are slightly more than 755 feet long, and it is just over 450 feet high.

The practice of burying kings in pyramids died out in the New Kingdom. At this time the pharaohs chose instead to have secret tombs in the Valley of the Kings at Luxor. It used to be thought that during the Old Kingdom, pyramids were built only for the kings and their families. However, recent excavations at Giza, the site of the Great Pyramid of Khufu, have shown that the workmen who built the pyramids sometimes also built mini-pyramids on top of their own tombs. There are also examples in the New Kingdom from a village called Deir el-Medina of private people still putting personal pyramids on their tombs.

CHAPTER 4

# BEAUTIFYING EGYPT

Building up Egypt required two things: materials and vision. While materials were limited, Snefru's imagination was wide enough that he could compensate for what was missing by participating in the international economy. In this way, Snefru made contributions to ancient Egyptian architecture and construction.

## WOOD

Snefru needed large supplies of wood, both to build more ships and for the construction of palaces and temples. Lebanon was famous for the fine quality of its woods, especially cedar wood. An image of the cedar tree is still on the Lebanese flag today. In the same year that he sent his army to Nubia, Snefru sent an expedition to Lebanon to buy timber.

This ancient Egyptian solar boat is made from Lebanon cedar wood. After being found in 1954, seventeen years passed before it was restored and put on display.

The Palermo stone records the building of the "wall of the Southland and Northland called 'Houses of Snefru,'" which was probably the foundation for a royal palace, and the "bringing of forty ships filled with cedar wood." This timber was put to good use. The records for the next year include the "building of a 100-cubit dewatowe ship of cedar wood." It is interesting that the construction of this ship was thought important enough to record, and it indicates that it was a very important vessel.

## EGYPTIAN BOATS AND SPIRITUALITY

Boats have strong symbolic meaning in ancient Egyptian religion. But in some cases, that meaning is unclear. It may be that a boat carries a corpse to its embalmment in the world of the living, or the boat may serve as a vessel in the underworld that brings the soul to the land of the gods, were it will become immortal. Since such a journey is meant to occur in a realm that the living cannot access, one would not see it move. Boats were also sometimes used by the Egyptian gods. Re was said to travel via boat across the sky and through creation.

Because of the very dry conditions of Egypt's climate and the preserving nature of sand, archaeologists have actually discovered and excavated some wooden boats made at this time. The most famous of these is a large cedar-wood rowing boat found next to the Great Pyramid of Khufu at Giza. In 1954 an Egyptian archaeologist named Kamal el-Mallakh uncovered a large oblong pit covered in stone slabs. When one of these was removed, a large cavity was revealed containing planks of wood, rope, matting, and oars. This proved to be the carefully dismantled remains of a boat. A team of restorers working under Hag Ahmed Youssef Moustafa took many years to put the boat back together, and it was finally placed on display for the public in 1971.

The boat is built from thick cedar planks, which were tied together with linen ropes. It has no mast or sail and was propelled by twelve oars. There were five oars down each side of the boat and two large oars at the stern (back) of the vessel, which were used to steer. On the deck there is a small wooden canopy at the bow (front) of the boat to protect a lookout or pilot from the sun. In the middle of the deck there is a large central cabin divided into two rooms. This is surrounded by a framework of wooden poles that would have supported a sunshade made from either linen or reed mats. The boat also contained a wooden gangplank that would have been extended for getting on and off. The vessel is 143 feet long, and must be very similar to that built by Snefru and described on the Palermo stone.

Snefru concentrated on expanding the capital city at Memphis. He built a fine new palace for himself and his family. The year after he built his big ship, he had enough cedar wood left to build huge wooden doors for the gates of his palace. The Palermo stone records the "erection of 'Exalted is the White Crown of Snefru upon the Southern Gate' and 'Exalted is the Red Crown of Snefru upon the Northern Gate.'"

## SNEFRU ENDURES

Snefru now had enough men and materials to continue the construction of his pyramid at Meidum. Some archaeologists used to think that the pyramid at Meidum was originally started by Snefru's father, Huni, for himself. This is mainly because a tomb for

This photo depicts the Pyramid Complex of Pepi I, located in Memphis, Egypt. Snefru's expansion of the capital had a notable impact on his successors.

Huni has not been found. However, the ancient name of Meidum was "Snefru Endures," and Snefru's name has been found written on scraps of stone that were instructions for workers at the site, so it seems likely that he started building the pyramid from the beginning.

The pyramid at Meidum started off as a step pyramid similar to that built by Djoser at Saqqara. During the first half of Snefru's reign, the first five of seven steps were built, before a change of plans led to these steps being covered over with eight bigger steps. At this point the pyramid was finished, and Snefru started to build another at Dahshur.

However, in the last years of his reign, workmen used stones to fill in the steps of the Meidum pyramid in order to turn it into what is known as a true pyramid, with smooth sloping slides.

The secret burial chamber was probably built first, with the pyramid then constructed on top. The burial chamber was originally entered through a small passage that began in the middle of the north wall of the pyramid. This passage descended through the body of the pyramid for 190 feet. At the bottom of the slope, there is a level corridor 31 feet long. At the end of this corridor a vertical shaft goes up about 20 feet into the floor of the burial chamber, which is 19 feet long and 8 feet wide.

There are two small rooms off the corridor that originally stored large stone slabs, which were to be dropped into place to block the passageway to the tomb once the king's body had been put inside. However, it seems that no one was ever actually buried in this pyramid. There is still some evidence of the pyramid complex, with traces of the mortuary temple, a satellite pyramid, and the causeway leading to the valley temple.

## SNEFRU'S BEREAVED PARENTHOOD

During the first part of Snefru's reign, when it was thought that he would be buried in the Meidum pyramid, at least two of Snefru's sons died. There are a number of mastaba tombs to the north of the pyramid, and these include the burial sites of two sons of Snefru called Nefermaat and Rahotep. Both these tombs are famous because of the objects found in them.

The tomb of Nefermaat and his wife, Atet, was decorated with colorful scenes of daily life for them and their children. These include pictures of men hunting birds in marshland and farmers ploughing and sowing seed. The tomb of Rahotep and his wife, Nofret, contained statues of the couple sitting down. These are made of limestone and are painted in a very lifelike way. Rahotep has reddish-brown skin, short black hair, and a little moustache. He is wearing a knee-length kilt and a necklace with a small heart charm on it. Nofret has pale yellowish skin and a black, shoulder-length wig. She is wearing a white dress with shoulder straps and a white cloak. She also wears a large colorful necklace

These statues depicting Prince Rahotep and his wife Nofret were found in a tomb to the north of the pyramid of Meidum.

that matches her headband. Both figures are wearing black eye makeup, which was used to help cut down the bright glare of the sun.

CHAPTER 5

# THE GOVERNMENT AND ITS POLICIES

The Egyptian government was all about managing people and resources. The main priorities of the government were to feed the people and complete building projects. The government also actively disregarded, if not directly harmed, those who didn't have a good relationship with the Egyptians, as Snefru would demonstrate.

## GOVERNMENT STRUCTURES

Evidence from private tombs surrounding the king's pyramids indicates that Snefru ran a highly efficient government. He appointed a large number of officials, who were mainly from his own extended family. He supervised their training and gave them presents of land on which to build their houses. He also paid for many of their burial sites in mastaba tombs around his three pyramids.

The central government was run from the king's palace complex at Memphis, where a series of official buildings surrounded the royal residence. The dual nature of the country was represented by certain dual titles and offices. Government departments included the treasury (with the power to

This illustration depicts priests and warriors that Snefru may have chosen to run his government.

tax), the armory, the granaries (also with the power to tax, in the form of expropriations of surplus grain from the countryside), and the department of public works, which concentrated on the construction of temples and palaces. The viziers were in charge of the legal side of government and the royal archives, but they were also directly answerable to Snefru.

Each major temple and royal mortuary complex was managed by a group of priests who were also under the direct command of the king. Egypt was divided into "nomes," or districts. In earlier periods these districts had been run as separate regions by local rulers. Snefru ensured that they were ruled as subordinate administrative districts by loyal members of his government who were called nomarchs.

## METHEN

One such nomarch who lived and died during the reign of Snefru was called Methen. His autobiography appears on the wall of his tomb at Saqqara, which was probably paid for by Snefru himself. The text illustrates the general organization of Snefru's government as well as listing many of Methen's own achievements. Methen lived and worked in the Nile Delta. His story shows his gradual rise from a scribe and overseer of a magazine, a storehouse, and a food distribution center, to become the local ruler of a number of towns in the delta and the Faiyum.

Methen starts off his story by listing what he inherited. "There were presented to him the things of his father, a judge and scribe called Anubisemonekh. There was no grain or anything of the house, but there were people and small cattle." This means that Methen was left a plot of land that had tenant farmers.

He then lists the progress of his career:

> He was made chief scribe of the provision magazine, and overseer of the things of the provision magazine. He became local governor of Xois and inferior field judge of Xois. He was appointed judge, he was made overseer of all the flax of the king. He was made ruler of southern Perked and deputy, he was made local governor of the people of Dep, palace ruler of Miper and Persepa and local governor of the Saite nome, ruler of the stronghold of Sent, ruler of Pershesthet, ruler of the towns of the palace, of the Southern Lake.

We can't identify exactly where all these places were, but it is clear that Methen had a very successful administrative career. It is also interesting to note that there is no indication that he came from a royal or even an important family. This suggests that it was possible for ambitious men from minor families

Mastabas like this structure in Saqqara, Egypt, often featured a tomb autobiography, which was the story of a government figure's achievements in life.

to rise through the ranks of Snefru's government.

Methen also describes the rewards given to him by Snefru throughout his career, which included a large house and grounds. "There were conveyed to him as a reward 200 *stat* of land...a mortuary offering of 100 loaves every day from the mortuary temple of the mother of the king's children, a house 200 *cubits* long and 200 *cubits* wide [235 square feet]...Very plentiful trees and vines were set out, a great quantity of wine was made there."

## CAMPAIGNS AGAINST NOMADS

Along with supervising

the construction of his pyramid and running his government, Snefru also had to concentrate on international affairs. The Palermo stone records that Snefru led campaigns against the Tjehenu, that is, the Libyans, who were a group of tribesmen who lived in the desert west of Egypt. The Tjehenu were nomadic, which means that they had not settled in one place, but lived in tents with their families and their possessions, including their animals, and moved from place to place. The Tjehenu were depicted as bearded and light skinned, sometimes with blue eyes. They are recognizable in Egyptian illustrations by blue tattoos, long cloaks, penis sheathes, pointed beards, long curls hanging on one side of their heads, and often with an ostrich feather in their hair.

In later periods of Egyptian history, the Tjehenu and other groups called the Tjemehu, the Meshwesh, and the Libu (the origin of the modern-day name, Libya) joined together to attack Egypt. But during the Old Kingdom, the Libyans did not pose any serious threat to the stability or safety of Egypt. However, Snefru organized a series of raids against these tribes to ensure that they kept away from the Nile Valley. Although the Libyans did not have many material goods to trade with the Egyptians, the feathers often worn in their hair shows that they had access to ostriches that also lived in the desert. The Egyptians wanted ostrich feathers from which to make fans and headdresses, and ostrich eggs for food. Ostrich eggs are very large, up to ten inches long, and one ostrich egg makes an omelette for twelve people.

## INVADING NUBIA

The closest country on Egypt's southern border was Nubia. Nubia occupied what is modern-day Sudan, as well as the southern part of Egypt now submerged under Lake Nasser. Egypt had been trading with Nubia from late predynastic times, as the Egyptians wanted the luxury goods native to that country, such as gold, ivory, and ebony. However, during the Old Kingdom, there was an increase in demand in Egypt for raw materials because of the strain of monumental building projects. This meant that Nubia was viewed as a source of goods to be taken rather than bought. Snefru was planning the construction of his enormous pyramid at Meidum, as well as new palaces and

## NUBIA AND EGYPT

The people of the territory occupying modern-day southern Egypt and north Sudan were a black people known as the Sudanese-Saharan Neolithic. The period of settling that they participated in started around 10,000 years ago and lasted until 3800 BCE.

Their society did not exist in a bubble. A new period, from 3800–3100 BCE, brought on the Nubians' first period of trading, putting them in regular contact with their northern Egyptian neighbors. In fact, Egypt conquered a northern portion of Nubia in 1950 BCE, seeking their gold and more extensive territory, and then lost it in around 1700 BCE. But Nubia rallied for the return and took over a weakened Egypt from 747–656 BCE, an era known as Egypt's twenty-fifth dynasty. And in late Nubian history, Egypt and Nubia banded together to take on foreign invaders, including the Persian and Roman empires.

temples in Memphis. These buildings all needed not only gold and precious materials to decorate them, but also large numbers of workers to undertake the task of construction.

Consequently, Snefru gathered an army by drawing from all the various local forces and also by recruiting some mercenaries. He appointed a commander who was known as the Overseer of Soldiers. This fighting force was then sent by boat upriver to Nubia. The Nubians were not actually any threat to the Egyptian state at this stage, and this action represented a policy of imperialist domination. It was the first of a number of vigorous military campaigns against Nubia where captives, cattle, and wood were taken. A special type of stone called diorite, used for making statues, was now available from Nubian quarries along the Nile. While in Nubia, the Egyptian army built a small settlement at Buhen near the second Nile cataract, about 250 miles south of the existing border at Aswan, where Huni had previously erected a fortress. The Palermo stone records that the Egyptians returned with 70,000 living prisoners and 200,000 large and small cattle.

These huge numbers illustrate the devastating effect that the Egyptian military action must have had on the population of Nubia. Whole villages were wiped out as men, women, and children were taken to Egypt. The men would have

# THE PALERMO STONE

The Palermo stone was a stele, a standing slab of stone inscribed with writing. It is our main source of information for the events of Snefru's reign. Unfortunately, it was smashed to pieces at some time in the past. The Palermo stone was erected during the Fifth Dynasty, at least one hundred years after the death of Snefru. It was inscribed with a set of royal annals, a list of the main events that happened in each year, going back to the beginning of Egyptian history. The object was originally over six feet high, but only a few fragments remain today. Some of these fragments list events that occurred during Snefru's reign.

This black diorite stele is the Palermo stone. The carvings on it describe the accomplishments of kings and their lineage.

worked in the army or on building projects, or would have been turned into farmers in the Nile Delta. The women and children would have been used as servants in houses or put to work in small businesses like bakeries or breweries. For those Nubians left behind, the loss of their cattle would have taken away one of their main sources of food and wealth.

## COPPER AND TURQUOISE

The Egyptians needed copper to make weapons for the army. The source for this metal was far off in the Sinai Desert. This area also contained turquoise, which was a blue or green gemstone that the Egyptians loved to use both in jewelry and to decorate small objects and pieces of furniture. One of the ancient Egyptians' favorite combinations of materials was green turquoise from the Sinai mountains, red carnelian from pebbles picked up in the eastern desert, and dark blue lapis lazuli imported from far away Afghanistan. These materials were strung together as beads for necklaces and bracelets or used as colorful inlays in gold headdresses and rings. Sometimes these stones were imitated by colored glass, which was done so successfully that it is often difficult for us to tell them apart. Both men and women wore jewelry throughout Egyptian history.

The background of this photo shows Mount Sinai, an abundant source of copper and turquoise for ancient Egyptians.

The mountains of the Sinai Desert had been a source of copper and turquoise since the predynastic period. The Egyptians sent expeditions of miners and quarry workers into the region. Getting to the Sinai involved a long trip, first overland across the eastern desert from the Nile Valley to the coast of the Red Sea, and then by ship to reach the west coast of the Sinai. Here the Egyptians would have unloaded their supplies of food, tools, and weapons, and also the donkeys that they brought with them to carry their tools to the turquoise quarry sites.

There is archaeological evidence from the period of Snefru's reign of campsites and mines at a site called Wadi Maghara, which is 140 miles west of Cairo. Copper-working also took place at this site, which indicates that the Egyptians probably also mined copper, as well as bought it from local tribesmen. There are also some fine pictures carved into rock walls of the pharaoh beating foreign captives. Snefru is shown wearing a crown and holding a mace above his head, ready to bring it down on a kneeling Bedouin tribesman who he is holding by the hair. An accompanying inscription lists the king's names and titles.

These pictures and inscriptions indicate that skilled craftsmen were included in the teams who went to the Sinai, and that they must have occasionally had spare time on their hands for artistic creation. On the return journey, the donkeys would carry the copper and turquoise to the ships, where everything would be loaded on board and sailed back to the east coast of Egypt.

CHAPTER 6

# THE PEOPLE OF THE PYRAMIDS

It was a long time before Snefru decided on an appropriate burial place, but building the pyramid of his dreams wasn't just a construction project. Every new pyramid required the creation of a new, temporary community, and a long-term commitment to maintaining the religious requirements of that type of structure.

## THE THREE PYRAMIDS

In the fifteenth year of his reign (2569 BCE), for some reason Snefru changed his mind about where he wanted to be buried, and he began to build another pyramid twenty-five miles farther north of Meidum at Dahshur. However, he was not happy with this new pyramid, and when it was finished he built yet another pyramid, again at Dahshur. This was not the end of the story, because after the third pyramid at Dahshur was finished, he sent workmen back to Meidum to complete the first one! All three pyramids were originally constructed out of local limestone, with highly polished white limestone slabs coating the outer surfaces. This outer layer was very attractive, but it has almost completely disappeared over the centuries as it was stripped away to be used for other building projects.

## THE BENT PYRAMID AT DAHSHUR

When Snefru started building his second pyramid at Dahshur, no one had ever made one with smooth sides like this before. It was started with very steep sides, but problems soon occurred. Cracks developed in the outer face and the internal corridors of the pyramid. To counter this, workmen built an extra layer around the outside of the pyramid, which made it bigger and gave it a gentler slope. However, fresh cracks still appeared, and so the top half of the slope was finished with an even shallower incline. This gave the side of the pyramid a curved or bent appearance as the slope changed.

The Bent Pyramid at Dahshur is the second pyramid that Snefru had built. Although the slope changes, the sides are still smooth.

This pyramid is also unique because it has not one but two secret burial chambers with two separate entrances, one on the north face and one on the east face. The north burial chamber and passage were probably constructed before the pyramid was built over it. The passage descends for 240 feet from the entrance. At the bottom there is a long narrow room with a 40-foot-high corbelled roof, which is formed from slabs of stone protruding from the walls and narrowing the roof space like an arch. The burial chamber is next to and above this room, and was probably originally reached by a ladder. This room also has a corbelled roof that is 57 feet high.

A second, similarly constructed burial chamber lies above and southeast of the first chamber. A roughly cut corridor now joins the two, but originally the only access to this second chamber was through a passage leading from an entrance on the west side of the pyramid. This passage slopes down for 212 feet before flattening out into a 66-foot-long corridor. This flat corridor contained two large stone slabs, called portcullises, which were meant to be slid across to block off the corridor once the burial was in place. One of these had been closed and disguised with plaster. This was to fool robbers into thinking that they had reached the end of the corridor. It is not known why this pyramid has two burial chambers and in fact there is no evidence that anyone was ever buried in this pyramid.

The pyramid complex is better preserved than the one at Meidum. We can see the remains of the mortuary temple at the foot of the eastern side of the pyramid, as well as the causeway leading to the valley temple. The valley temple itself was vandalized and destroyed at some time in the past, but some of the carvings from the walls are quite well preserved.

## THE RED PYRAMID AT DAHSHUR

Perhaps he was not satisfied with the various changes to the design of the Bent Pyramid, because before it was even completed Snefru embarked on the construction of yet another pyramid at Dahshur. From the beginning, this one was constructed with a gentler slope, more like the upper section of the bent pyramid. Today it is known as the Red Pyramid because of the reddish color of the limestone used in the core. The white limestone surface that originally covered the pyramid has long since worn away. The pyramid was originally 343 feet high, and each side was 722 feet long at the base.

A corridor starting in the north face of the pyramid descends for 206 feet through the core. This flattens out into a corridor 24 feet long that enters the first chamber, which is an oblong room 27 feet by 12 feet with a corbeled roof 40 feet tall. A short passage then leads to a second room, again

The third and final pyramid that Snefru had built was the Red Pyramid, also in Dahshur.

with a 40 foot roof. A secret passage starts 25 feet above the floor high up in the wall of this second chamber. It is 24 feet long and leads into the burial chamber. This is a big room measuring 14 feet by 28 feet, and it is 50 feet tall.

After the funeral, the entrance to the secret passage would have been disguised to look like the rest of the blank wall. Unfortunately, however, at some point in the past this passage was discovered by tomb robbers, and when excavators cleared the burial chamber in 1950, all they found were a few fragments of human remains. Nevertheless, it is thought that Snefru was probably buried in this pyramid, and it is possible that these are the remains of his mummy. There is some evidence of the pyramid complex, but the mortuary temple and the valley temple were hurriedly finished, suggesting that Snefru died before they were completed.

## PYRAMID TOWNS

Pyramid towns grew up around each pyramid as it was constructed. To begin with, the many thousands of people who were building the whole pyramid complex needed housing while working on the construction. This included the men who cut and shaped the blocks, the men who dragged them into place, the architects and designers who checked that everything was working properly, and all the special tradesmen who looked after all the tools that were used, mending those that were broken and constantly making new ones. Some of these people would have been based near the pyramids all year round, and some would have come only during the Inundation season, when they couldn't work on their own farms at home.

These towns also contained all the other people who looked after the workers. These included bakers to make all the bread and beer that the workers ate and drank. Evidence from the pyramid town of Snefru's son Khufu also shows that masses of fish were eaten, and a factory site has been found were many thousands of catfish were cleaned, skinned, and had their bones taken out. There were also many butchers to kill and process animals that were brought to the site for food. Many of the workmen brought their wives and children to live with them, and so all the activities of a normal town took place around the pyramid, with markets, schools, pottery factories, and temples for worship. Building a

## GRAVE ROBBERS

Political unrest in Egypt during the second decade of the twenty-first century has exacerbated the age-old problem of grave robbing. Since former president Hosni Mubarak stepped down from office in 2011, tomb raiders have worked with little resistance from the government. They have pillaged sites like the pyramids at Dahshur and sold their artifacts on the black market, possibly never to be recovered by Egypt again.

While unlikely, recovery is not impossible. The Egyptian government may initiate the recovery process by registering the full inventory of missing relics as stolen, thus allowing them to reclaim artifacts as they appear in legitimate markets or museums.

pyramid was quite dangerous work. Workers could fall off the pyramid or the ramps, or be crushed by one of the huge blocks, and archeaologists have found large graveyards connected to these pyramid towns. Common people were not mummified at this period, and there are many hundreds of skeletons from the town by Khufu's pyramid. Analysis of these bones has shown that many of the workmen suffered from arthritis and joint disease, especially in their backs. This is not a surprise if you consider the amount of hard manual labor involved in pyramid building.

After the pyramid was completed, many of the workmen either moved on to the next large building project or went home to their villages and farms. However, a group of people stayed and lived near the pyramid in order to run the cult or religious services that took place every day. Scraps of papyrus found near the pyramid of the Fifth Dynasty pharaoh Neferirkara give some clues of what these priests actually did. There was a permanent group of priests known as servants of the god

as well as five groups of priests, each divided into two smaller groups, who took turns serving in the pyramid complex for one month every ten months. This meant that for the rest of the year these people could go to their homes and work there.

These are tombs of pyramid builders. A project of such massive proportions was liable to cause many deaths.

Their jobs included assisting in the daily rituals in the temple and looking after all the provisions that came to the pyramids. The rituals included washing and dressing statues of the king, and then chanting prayers in front of the statues while burning incense. Food and drink were then offered to the statues. After a short while, the sacred essence of this was thought to go magically into the statues of the king, and so the actual provisions were taken away and eaten by the priests. All this took place up to five times a day.

## LOOKING AFTER THE PYRAMID COMPLEXES

One of the problems that Snefru had to think about was who was going to look after his pyramid complexes after he died. The priests who worked at the pyramid temple were meant to take offerings of food and drink to the Ka, or soul, of the king every day, forever. This meant that the offerings had to be provided, and the priests had to be paid, as did the gardeners, cleaners, and other people who looked after the complex. They were all paid with goods rather than money. This might include bread and beer, meat and vegetables, and new clothes and shoes.

The pharaoh could have hoped that future kings would continue to pay all these people. However, a safer way to ensure continuing prayers at his temple was to set up a system of support that did not rely on the good will of his descendants. The pharaoh was the biggest landowner in Egypt, and owned large numbers of farms and estates all over Egypt. Snefru solved the problem by giving a large number of these estates to his pyramids. This meant that instead of having a human landlord, all the farmers who worked on these lands paid their rent to the pyramid in the form of goods that they had produced.

Rows of illustrations on the walls of Snefru's valley temple show exactly how this happened. Each estate is represented as a woman holding a tray full of offerings, with the name and location of each estate written in front. This system shows us that each pyramid created employment for many thousands of people. Resources belonging to the king in the form of food and drink produced on different farms all over the country were brought to one central place. Here they were distributed to all the workers as payment for their services. Consequently, the pyramids represent not only an incredible example of mass organization of people and materials, but also a very successful form of an economy based on the redistribution of goods. We don't know how many people it actually took to build each pyramid, but it has been estimated that between 20,000 and 30,000 men worked in three-month shifts, meaning that nearly 100,000 people were employed each year. They, and their wives and families, were thus directly bound to the power of the king.

CHAPTER 7

# DEATH AND LEGACIES

Snefru's death left Khufu, his son, in charge, and would eventually leave the archaeological community mystified. Investigations eventually revealed significant insight into what probably happened, and what Snefru was like. And close attention to detail revealed some answers, even if those who looked could never be sure of everything.

## THE RUSE OF HETEPHERES

After a long and successful reign, King Snefru died in 2560 BCE. He was succeeded by his son Khufu, who is still famous today as the builder of the Great Pyramid at Giza, which is one of the seven wonders of the ancient world.

The Sphinx (*foreground*) and the Great Pyramid of Giza (*background*) were built relatively shortly after Snefru's reign.

Although archaeologists have not been able to find much real evidence of the burial of Snefru, a lucky accident revealed a wonderful group of objects originally belonging to his wife Hetepheres. In 1925, a team from Harvard University was working at the Great Pyramid at Giza built by King Khufu, the son of Snefru and Hetepheres. One day a photographer's tripod "struck a curious patch of plaster." This turned out to conceal the top of a burial shaft. Further investigation revealed a hidden burial chamber containing a sarcophagus (a box to put a coffin in) and various pieces of furniture and funeral equipment. Many of the objects were originally covered in gold foil but were in a very poor state because all the wood parts had long since rotted away. However, after years of painstaking reconstruction, we can now see the furniture that belonged to Hetepheres, including a bed, chairs, boxes, and an elaborate frame to hold up a tent around her bed. Inscriptions on many of the objects show that they had been given to Hetepheres by Snefru and Khufu.

This discovery created a couple of mysteries. First, why was the wife of Snefru buried with her son at Giza rather than with her husband at Dahshur?

## THE FOURTH DYNASTY CONTINUES

Although Khufu is most well-known for the Great Pyramid at Giza, commissioning that work was only the beginning of his reign. Like his father, Khufu would rule for twenty-four years and lead in several victorious military excursions against Nubia and Libya. But not much else is known about him.

The following ruler of Egypt, Djedefre, was an even more obscure figure. Did he kill his brother, the original heir to the throne? Was his reign eight years, twenty, or some number in between? And how did his successors feel about his legacy? Several statues of Djedefre were defaced sometime after his reign, possibly immediately after. Was this done by his successors to show their disapproval?

Similar uncertainty exists for the history of the remaining rulers of this dynasty.

Second, if this was indeed the burial place of Hetepheres, then why, when the sarcophagus was opened, was it empty?

The excavator of the tomb, George Reisner, suggested answers to both these questions. He thought that Hetepheres and her furniture had originally been buried in a satellite pyramid next to the Red Pyramid at Dahshur. However, soon after she was buried her tomb was broken into and ransacked by thieves who stole her body. When news of this reached the vizier (the governor of this area) he panicked. As the person in charge of security, he would be in serious trouble if the new king, Khufu, heard that the body of his mother had been stolen. Consequently, the vizier ordered the lid put back on the empty sarcophagus, and he pretended to Khufu that Hetepheres's body was still inside the box! Everybody then agreed that it would be safer for her burial to be transferred to Giza and re-hidden in a new tomb.

## EXAMINING THE EVIDENCE

We also have reason to believe that a different Giza site, tomb G7000-X, may have been Hetepheres' original burial site. The inside of an alabaster box or chest hidden on a small shelf was divided into four compartments. One of these contained dry organic matter in the bottom, and the other three had a yellowish liquid. This liquid was analyzed and proved to be natron, a material used for embalming, as well as the remains of the internal organs of the queen.

The finds in the Great Pyramid are the best evidence that we have for furniture and funerary equipment during the Old Kingdom. They were all beautifully made and decorated, and show a high degree of skill in carpentry and gold working. The canopy is an example of painting from the predynastic period onward. It was designed to be hung

This satellite pyramid is believed to be the original resting place of Queen Hetepheres. Unfortunately, it was robbed shortly after entombment.

with mats or curtains, both to ensure privacy and to keep mosquitoes away while sleeping. A box for storing the curtains was found next to the poles of the canopy. The bed had an inlaid footboard and a silver covered headrest. Egyptian beds sloped down towards the foot end. Two chairs were found, but only one could be completely reconstructed. This has a wide, low seat with decorated side and back panels. There is another chair on poles for carrying the queen, and there are also various boxes covered with elaborate decorations. One of these contained twenty silver bracelets arranged in two rows. These are all decorated with butterflies made of blue lapis lazuli, red carnelian, and green turquoise. The label on the box reads "box containing rings" and "Mother of the King of Upper and Lower Egypt Hetepheres," and a painting of Hetepheres from the back of the other incomplete chair shows her wearing rows of bracelets just like these.

## A TALE OF SNEFRU

A story told nearly a thousand years after his time illustrates that later generations remembered Snefru as a kind and happy king. This was written down on a document now called the Westcar Papyrus.

One day King Snefru was bored and wandered through all the rooms of the palace in search

This painting on papyrus depicts an Egyptian king and one of his wives in a boat on the Nile River.

of something to do. He summoned one of the men who worked in his household, saying "Go, bring me the chief lector priest, the scribe of books Djadja-em-ankh." The tale says,

"He was brought to him straight away. His majesty said to him 'I have gone through all the rooms of the palace in search of relaxation and found none.' Djadja-em-ankh said to him 'May your majesty proceed to the lake of the palace. Fill a boat with all the beautiful girls of your palace. Your majesty's heart will be refreshed by seeing them row

> up and down. As you observe the fine nesting places of your lake, as you observe its beautiful fields and shores, your heart will be refreshed.'"

The king was very pleased by this idea, and replied, "Let there be brought to me twenty women with the shapeliest bodies, breasts and braids, who have not yet given birth. Also let there be brought to me twenty nets and give these nets to the women in place of their clothes." The girls did as they were told, and "they rowed up and down, and his majesty's heart was happy seeing them row." However, one of the girls dropped her new turquoise necklace over the side of the boat, and when Snefru said "Row! I shall replace it for you," the girl replied that "I prefer my thing to one like it." So the king summoned Djadja-em-ankh once more, and the priest cast a spell which "placed one side of the lake's water upon the other," and he then found the pendant lying on a stone on the bottom of the lake. The story finishes with "His majesty spent the day feasting with the entire palace. Then he rewarded the chief lector priest Djadja-em-ankh with all good things."

**cubit** Approximately the length of a man's forearm, the main unit of distance measurement in ancient Egypt.

**dynasty** A period of time in ancient Egyptian history specific to a single royal family or a single capital, or some other factor.

**Inundation** The season of the annual flooding of the Nile, which took place between June and September.

***Ka*** The life force that was born at the same time as a person and existed beyond death.

**king lists** A group of carvings or paintings listing the names and titles of former kings in succession.

**logographic** Describes a style of writing that represents a word or a phrase.

**Lower Egypt** The northern half of the country stretching from Memphis to the Mediterranean coast.

**Maat** A goddess who embodied aspects of truth, justice, and harmony in the universe, and whose power regulated the seasons and the movement of the sun, the moon, and the stars.

**mastaba** A type of rectangular tomb used by wealthy private individuals during the Old Kingdom.

**Medjay** Nomadic group from the eastern deserts of Nubia who were employed in the Egyptian army.

**Memphis** Capital city of Ancient Egypt, close to modern-day Cairo.

**nomes** The forty-two administrative districts or provinces of Egypt.

**Nubia** The region immediately south of Ancient Egypt.

**pharaoh** New Kingdom term for Egyptian king that came from *per-aa* or "Great House," the name of the palace.

**sarcophagus** A container that holds a coffin that ancient Egyptian kings were often placed in.

**Upper Egypt** The southern half of the country stretching from Memphis to Aswan.

**vizier** The chief minister of the government who was based at Memphis and was in charge of the supervision of state building projects, taxation, and the law.

American Research Center in Egypt (US Office)
8700 Crownhill Boulevard, Suite 507
San Antonio, TX 78209-1130
(210) 821-7000
Website: http://www.arce.org/main
Creates opportunities for supporting scholarship, training, and conservation efforts in Egypt by utilizing relationships with antiquities governance organizations.

Ancient Egypt Research Associates
26 Lincoln Street, Suite 5
Brighton, MA 02135
(617) 783-0737
Website: http://www.aeraweb.org
This international community supports research, education, conservation, and training to reveal the history and culture of ancient Egypt.

Archaeological Institute of America Headquarters
Boston University
656 Beacon Street, 6th Floor
Boston, MA 02215-2006
(617) 353-8708
Website: https://www.archaeological.org
This organization hosts lectures, workshops, and tours, and builds databases that share information on Egyptian cultural and natural heritage.

Canadian Museum of History
100 Laurier Street
Gatineau, QC K1A 0M8
Canada
(800) 555-5621
Website: http://www.historymuseum.ca
This museum hosts exhibitions and activities, and enables research in topics that include Egyptian history and archaeology.

Rosicrucian Egyptian Museum
1660 Park Avenue
San Jose, CA 95191
Website: http://www.egyptianmuseum.org
In addition to its exhibitions, this museum runs special events and a junior archaeologist training program for children and young adults, and its website also offers resources for education.

The Society for the Study of Egyptian Antiquities
PO Box 19004 Walmer
360A Bloor Street W
Toronto, ON M5S 3C9
Canada
(647) 520-4339
Website: http://www.thessea.org/index.php
This organization supports professional and non-professional Egyptology studies, and sponsors and promotes archaeological research in Egypt.

## WEBSITES

Because of the changing nature of internet links, Rosen Publishing has developed an online list of websites related to the subject of this book. This site is updated regularly. Please use this link to access this list:

http://www.rosenlinks.com/LANW/snefru

Depauw, Mark, and Sandra Coussement, ed. *Identifiers and Identification Methods in the Ancient World: Legal Documents in Ancient Societies III* (Orientalia Lovaniensia Analecta). Leuven, Belgium: Peeters Publishing, 2014.

Der Manuelian, Peter, and Thomas Schneider. *Towards a New History for the Egyptian Old Kingdom: Perspectives on the Pyramid Age*. Leiden, Netherlands: Brill Academic Publishers, 2015.

Fletcher, Joann. *The Story of Egypt: The Civilization that Shaped the World*. New York, NY: Pegasus Books, 2016.

Ikram, Salima. *Egyptian Bioarchaeology: Humans, Animals, and the Environment*. Leiden, Netherlands: Sidestone Press, 2015.

Kobusiewicz, Michał. *The Production, Use and Importance of Flint Tools in the Archaic Period and the Old Kingdom in Egypt*. Oxford, UK: Archaeopress Archaeology, 2016.

McFarlane, A., and A. L. Mourad, eds. *Behind the Scenes: Daily Life in Old Kingdom Egypt* (The Australian Centre for Epyptology Studies). North Ryde, Australia: Australian Centre for Egyptology, 2013.

Moeller, Nadine. *The Archaeology of Urbanism in Ancient Egypt: From the Predynastic Period to the End of the Middle Kingdom*. Cambridge, UK: Cambridge University Press, 2016.

Ryholt, Kim, and Gojko Barjamovic, eds. *Problems of Canonicity and Identity Formation in Ancient Egypt and Mesopotamia* (Carsten Niebuhr Institute Publications). Copenhagen, Denmark: Museum Tusculanum Press, 2016.

Swinton, Joyce. *Dating the Tombs of the Egyptian Old Kingdom*. Oxford, UK: Archaeopress Archaeology, 2014.

Tignor, Robert L. *Egypt: A Short History*. Princeton, NJ: Princeton University Press, 2011.

Warden, Leslie Anne. *Pottery and economy in Old Kingdom Egypt*. Leiden, Netherlands: Brill Academic Publishers, 2013.

*Al Jazeera*. "Hosni Mubarak Resigns as President." February 11, 2011. http://www.aljazeera.com/news/middleeast/2011/02/201121125158705862.html.

Baraniuk, Chris. "Why Do We Still Not Know What's Inside the Pyramids?" British Broadcasting Corporation, November 13, 2015. http://www.bbc.com/future/story/20151113-why-do-we-still-not-know-whats-inside-the-pyramids.

Bluffton University. "Solar Boat/Funerary Boat of Cheops (Khufu)" Retrieved October 27, 2016. http://www.bluffton.edu/homepages/facstaff/SULLIVANM/egypt/giza/boat/boat.html.

Breasted, James. *Ancient Records of Egypt Vol. I: The First through Seventeenth Dynasties*, Chicago, IL: University of Chicago Press, 2001.

*Egyptian Art in the Age of the Pyramids*. New York, NY: Exhibition Catalogue, Metropolitan Museum of Art, 1999.

Fakhry, Ahmed. *The Monuments of Sneferu at Dahshur*. (2 vols.). Cairo, Egypt: General Organisation for Government Printing Offices, 1959 & 1961.

Hayes, William. *The Scepter of Egypt I: From the Earliest Times to the End of the Middle Kingdom*. New York, NY: Metropolitan Museum of Art, 1990.

Hobson, Christine. *The World of the Pharaohs: A Complete Guide to Ancient Egypt*. New York, NY: Thames and Hudson, 1987.

Lehner, Mark. *The Complete Pyramids*. London, England

& New York, NY: Thames & Hudson, 1997.

Lichtheim, Miriam. *Ancient Egyptian Literature Volume I: The Old and Middle Kingdoms*. Berkeley, CA: UCLA Press, 1975.

Lorenzi, Rosella. "Great Pyramid at Giza May Contain Secret Passage." Discovery Channel, November 10, 2015. http://www.discovery.com/dscovrd/adrenaline/great-pyramid-at-giza-may-contain-secret-passage/.

Lyon, Alissa. "Djedefre." Michigan State University, October 9, 2014, http://anthropology.msu.edu/anp455-fs14/2014/10/09/djedefre/.

Reisner, George, and William Stevenson Smith. *A History of the Giza Necropolis Volume II*. Cambridge, MA: Harvard Press, 1955.

Salloum, Raniah. "Tomb Raiders Exploit Chaos in Egypt." Spiegel Online, July 31, 2013. http://www.spiegel.de/international/world/tomb-raiders-in-egypt-exploit-political-chaos-to-steal-antiquities-a-914058.html.

The University of North Carolina at Chapel Hill. "Egyptian Iconography." Retrieved October 25, 2016. https://www.unc.edu/courses/2005fall/art/080a/001/EGYPT%20INTRO%20&%20MISC/egyptian%20iconography.htm.

*The World Factbook 2016–17*. Washington, DC: Central Intelligence Agency, 2013.

## K



## L



## M



## N



## O



## P

## R



## S



## T

# ABOUT THE AUTHOR

Beatriz Santillian earned her BA in English in 2003 and her PhD in history in 2009. She is a fan of all things to do with ancient history and loves to learn about artifacts from the past. Santillian writes on topics to do with culture, technology, and change, and she also writes software in her spare time. She lives in Rochester, New York, with her daughter.

Susanna Thomas has a BA in Egyptian archaeology from University College, London, and was awarded a PhD from Liverpool University in 2000. She has worked sites all over Egypt, including in the Valley of the Kings, and runs excavations at Tell Abqa'in in the western Delta. She is particularly interested in vitreous materials and trade in the late Bronze Age.

## PHOTO CREDITS

Cover, p. 3 JMCC1/Wikimedia Commons/File:Snofru Eg Mus Kairo 2002 b.jpg/CC BY-SA 3.0; cover (background) WitR/Shutterstock.com; p. 7 Apic/Hulton Archive/Getty Images; p. 13 Sandro Vannini/Corbis Documentary/Getty Images; p. 16 © iStockphoto.com/enviromantic; pp. 20–21, 43 Universal History Archive/Universal Images Group/Getty Images; pp. 22, 70 DEA Picture Library/De Agostini/Getty Images; pp. 26, 58, 76–77 Werner Forman/Universal Images Group/Getty Images; p. 29 Museum of Fine Arts, Boston, Massachusetts, USA/Museum purchase with funds by exchange from the Egypt Exploration Fund by subscription/Bridgeman Images; pp. 32–33 Mountainpix/Shutterstock.com; pp. 36–37 De Agostini/C. Sappa/De Agostini Picture Library/Getty Images; pp. 40–41 Leonid Andronov/Shutterstock.com; pp. 46–47 Medioimages/Photodisc/Thinkstock; pp. 50, 54–55 DEA/A. Dagli Orti/De Agostini/Getty Images; pp. 60–61 Hulton Archive/Getty Images; pp. 64–65 Toño Labra/age footstock/SuperStock; pp. 72–73 DEA/G. Sioen/De Agostini/Getty Images; p. 80 Nestor Noci/Shutterstock.com; pp. 84–85 DEA/S. Vannini/De Agostini/Getty Images; p. 90 Volgablue/iStock/Thinkstock; p. 94 Baloncici/iStock/Thinkstock; pp. 96–97 Strakovskaya/Shutterstock.com; interior pages background images © iStockphoto.com/kikkalek5050 (sky), Triff/Shutterstock.com (map).

Designer: Brian Garvey; Editor: Bernadette Davis; Photo Researcher: Sherri Jackson